Insider Guide

AF789050

Killer Investment Banking Resumes! The WetFeet Insider Guide

2004 Edition

WetFeet®

Helping you make smarter career decisions.

WetFeet Inc.

609 Mission Street

Suite 400

San Francisco, CA 94105

Phone: (415) 284-7900 or 1-800-926-4JOB

Fax: (415) 284-7910

E-mail: info@wetfeet.com

Website: www.wetfeet.com

Killer Investment Banking Resumes! The WetFeet Insider Guide

ISBN: 1-58207-312-0

WetFeet®

Table of Contents

WetFeet®

Investment Banking Resumes at a Glance

The Resume's Raison d'Etre

- 30 seconds or less to get you to the interview room—or not
- Guide for subsequent discussion in your interview
- Will NOT get you a job

Cover Letters

- Do not play a major role
- Can do more harm than good

Anatomy of the Resume

- Content: Education, Experience, Other
- Format: clean, clear, conservative
- Don'ts: Career Objective, colored paper, lies

The Big Four Characteristics Sought by Banking

- Quantitative/analytical ability
- Drive for results
- Communication skills
- Team player mentality

The Big Four Characteristics Sought by Sales & Trading

- Negotiation skills
- Intellect
- Communication skills/relationship building
- Power of persuasion

Telling Your Story

Think about things you've done that demonstrate the Big Four characteristics—remember, it doesn't have to have been in an investment banking context

Overview

You're dying to get an interview with Goldman, Morgan Stanley, or Merrill. The resume submission deadline is only days away. You know that hundreds of your classmates are vying for a spot on the same crowded interview schedules. How will your resume stand out among the crowd? You know there's no way you'll be able to add another extracurricular presidency to your list of "Other Activities" by next week. Even you can't read your resume for more than 10 seconds without your eyes rolling into the back of your head. Will you have enough points to bid for a spot on all of those schedules? Ahhhh!

Take a deep breath. We're going to help you get some of the interviews without having to bid all of those points. Of course, it goes without saying that competition is tough. With corporate scandals and a lackluster economy, many banks are cutting their hiring numbers—making it even tougher. Take heart. The jobs are there. But only for those who can show in 30 seconds or less that they are worth a second look. Yes, that's right: 30 seconds. That's the most time any resume reviewer will spend on the initial review of your resume. That means you need to do the best possible job of presenting your skills and capabilities in a powerfully presented resume. By identifying and presenting your quantitative/analytical skills, your drive for results and your teamwork abilities in a format that's easy to read and understand, you will improve your chances of at least getting into the interview room.

This guide is designed to help you do the best possible job of presenting your qualifications for a career in either banking (corporate finance or mergers and acquisitions) or sales and trading (capital markets). Although it won't land you a job at a prestigious firm—there's a lot more to getting a job offer than sending a good resume—it should give you insight into how the resume review process works, and what firms are seeking. It is designed to help college and graduate students (or anyone else pondering a career in investment banking) present themselves in the best possible light to recruiters, resume readers, and interviewers from the top firms in the United States.

We interviewed insiders from some of the industry's elite firms (including Lehman, UBS PaineWebber, and Merrill) to find out exactly what they look for in resumes and cover letters. Although there was some variation between companies, the comments were remarkably consistent: Resume content is important, but packaging also plays an important role for investment banks. This guide will show you how to get a handle on both as you prepare to write your resume. We start by looking at how firms review resumes (and cover letters). We continue with a description of the standard investment banking resume and suggestions about structure and format, after which we tell you how to turn your experiences and education into something that will appeal to the resume reviewer. Finally, we review real resumes and give suggestions for improvement. Are you ready to begin? Let's dive in!

The Bottom Line

Remember this: Your resume will not get you an investment banking job. However, it is essential to getting your foot in the door of a top firm and putting your candidacy into serious consideration. *At best,* resume readers spend 30 seconds reviewing a resume the first time. In 30 seconds, an excellent resume conveys an image of who you are, what you're capable of, and how you have used your abilities to accomplish results. It indicates that you know yourself well and have a firm grasp on what you bring to the table. Or it doesn't. Although insiders tell us that "there isn't one right answer" to the question of how to create a good resume (good news for most of us!), they say the best resumes are concise, results-oriented, and very clearly presented. The correct structure can make you a more likely interview target and can even help you sail more smoothly through the interview process. Through conversations with insiders and reviews of resume books, we found that a lot of aspiring investment bankers don't understand this. This guide will help you get ahead of them in line.

Note: In this guide, we use *investment banking* as an umbrella term. For our purposes, it includes, corporate finance, mergers and acquisitions, debt and equity sales and trading. You may want to read our Insider Guide to *Careers in Investment Banking* for in-depth descriptions of each area.

Firm's-Eye View

How Resumes Are Used in the I-Banking Recruiting Process

Before you can write a killer resume, it's probably a good idea to know exactly what happens to it after it leaves your hands. Our investment banking insiders tell us that your resume and cover letter have an important but limited role in the selection and evaluation process. Here's how they fit in.

Most firms' recruiting teams are made up of members that are almost always based in their headquarters who then team up with colleagues in the appropriate regional offices. Recruiting teams are usually made up of bankers from several levels (ranging from undergrad hires to MDs) as well as a recruiting coordinator or manager from human resources. At the larger firms, most team members will be alums of your school. At least one of the team members will probably be a recent graduate of your school. This helps the recruiting teams distinguish real and inflated points on a resume, and make informed judgments of your credentials.

Your resume will likely be read by at least two team members who are appointed to review independently submitted resumes and resume books from target schools. As one insider puts it, "We're looking for a reason to ding them."

The next step at many firms is for the recruiting team to discuss the top candidates and decide who will receive interview invites. In these sessions, the initial reviewer might be asked to describe the candidate, tell his or her "story," and explain what is compelling about the candidate. In some cases, the team captain MD will do a final resume review and make interview decisions, either after the group discussion or in lieu of it.

Remember, team members responsible for recruiting are usually busy juggling several deals. They tend to review hundreds of resumes at a time and have very little time to spend on each one. Knowing this will help you understand just how forgettable any single resume can be—and just how compelling yours has got to be to stand out.

From the firm's point of view, the resume has one primary purpose: to help determine which candidates merit interviews. A well-executed resume will increase your chances of getting an interview, but it won't get you a job offer. Additionally, your resume will often serve as the basis for an ongoing evaluation of your candidacy. Each person who interviews you will probably have a copy of your resume and often a copy of the comments of those who have already interviewed you. Your interviewer will use the resume to identify areas to explore during the interview. Weaknesses or holes will be probed, strengths will be questioned, and anything that seems suspect will definitely be tested.

Each firm has its own strategy for navigating the resume flow—you'll want to do your homework on their respective businesses, cultures, and staffing approaches to get a sense of their priorities. Within each organization, however, there are obvious "breeds" of resume reviewer. Based on our research, we've grouped them as three different species: general scanners, spike seekers, and idealists. You won't know which type will pick up your resume. However, as you figure out how to present your skills, it's useful to know how various reviewers sort through their stacks.

General scanners. General scanners have a broad list of attributes in mind and spend a minimal amount of time matching resumes to their criteria. Usually, they start by doing a quick scan, looking for the obvious scoop on the person: Did they go to a top school? Have they worked for good companies? What functional knowledge do they have? It's really helpful if this information comes immediately to the eye. If they like what they see, then they'll read through the entire resume. This approach is fairly typical of the way an investment banking team member reads resumes.

Spike seekers. Spike seekers love highlights. They're looking for the one thing that will make this person stand out. Several reviewers say that they need to be able to tell a compelling story about a candidate during resume review sessions. Often the story will be about how one or two very strong and unique traits come through clearly in the resume.

Idealists. Some reviewers have an ideal in mind before they start reading, and look for how well a resume measures up against it. For example, they look for elements of the "Big Four" characteristics: analytical skills, academics (a 3.8 GPA or above and mention of honors), and a team-type activity such as sports or community involvement. One insider says, "I look for basic smarts, a team player with leadership skills. The captain of the lacrosse team with a high GPA." Other idealists have a preference for one thing they'd like to see on a resume, based on their own experience as well as their observations of how past hires have performed. These individuals are the most difficult to please, because they each look for different things.

Common Characteristics of a Successful Candidate

Although we've identified some very specific methods of the resume review, we found overwhelming similarity in what reviewers consider to be important resume attributes. Most look for three or four required elements (what we call the "Big Four") and several others that point to a candidate's likely success as an investment banker. As a general rule, candidates are not expected to excel in each of the required areas, but should have checks in all of them and show outstanding capability in at least one. The characteristics identified most frequently areas follows.

For Banking

- Quantitative/analytical ability
- Drive for results
- Communication skills
- Team player mentality

For Sales and Trading

- Negotiation skills
- Intellect
- Communication skills/relationship building
- Power of persuasion

Additional Important Factors

- Relevant industry or functional experience (very important for experienced hires)
- Leadership capability or potential
- Knowledge of financial services
- Ability to balance multiple responsibilities
- Client oriented

- Top schools
- Interesting activities

Some of the above items aren't on an official resume review list, but they influence whether resumes are selected. Firms weigh these items differently, depending on what type of work they do and how they deploy junior-level staff.

How Cover Letters Are Used in the I-Banking Recruiting Process

Insiders overwhelmingly indicated that little, if any, attention is paid to cover letters. Sometimes they're read, sometimes not. Because of this, a cover letter is almost more of a courtesy than a necessity (though we would not advise submitting a resume through the mail without attaching a cover letter). One insider says, "We do look at them, but we skim [rather than read] them."

Anatomy of a Resume

The first step in preparing your resume is to understand (and accept) the basic rules, so that your presentation won't get you thrown out of the game. There are two areas in which you should conform to standard practice: packaging and content. Resume readers prefer to focus more on content, but it's format that enables them to pick out useful information quickly. To assure a good read, both content and format must be in top shape. We discuss each in greater detail below, but as a general rule, these are not places to push the envelope. Remember, resume readers work 60- to 100-hour weeks. They are just looking for an excuse to throw your resume into the circular file. Few of them will give you extra credit for using bright blue paper or putting cartoons on your resume. If anything, this will get you dinged.

Decide on Your Focus

First things first, you'll need to customize your resume for banking or sales and trading. If you are an undergrad or first-year MBA, it's okay to look at both areas. However, we suggest you target your resume toward your top choice. If you are a second-year MBA or experienced hire, it's not okay to pursue both areas. If you do, you'll come across as being unfocused. If you really want that interview, take time to write a solid resume that's relevant to the type of work you are pursuing. The most important thing to do when writing your resume is to be concise.

Resume Sequence

Your resume should have three sections: Education, Experience and Other. In terms of sequence, you should lead with your strength. If you're a student, and particularly if you're from a top-ranked school, start your resume off with Education. Experienced professionals (those a few years or more out of school) should always lead with and emphasize Experience. As your school days become more distant, they become less relevant and firms become much more interested in your professional experience than in the fact that you were editor of your school newspaper. The Other section should always be last.

Do not include Career Objective, Career Summary, or another general overview section as all of these are superfluous. After all, the resume itself is a summary of your experience, skills, and accomplishments. And as for the Career Objective, that's an obvious one to the resume reviewer: If you've sent your resume for consideration, then it's a no-brainer that you're looking for a job with that firm. So leave it out.

Resume Content

Education

This section might be more aptly titled "Education and Academic Achievement." Information here should include schools attended, degrees conferred and when, and other information regarding your academic achievement, including GPA, SAT/GRE/GMAT scores, scholarships and awards earned, honor society memberships, class ranking, etc. List only those things that showcase your strengths. A 3.5 GPA isn't likely to impress anyone, nor is a 600 on the GMAT. These are perfectly respectable statistics, but they aren't going to wow the reader, so you might as well save the space for other details.

Coming from a top-ranked school is helpful, but it will hardly qualify you as unique at any of the best firms. While there is more leeway in the college ranks, the "top school" sentiment is echoed at most major firms as a quick and easy way to separate the wheat from the chaff. If you're from a less well-known institution, whether it's a college or a graduate school, be prepared to show your strengths in other critical areas because your resume is likely to be a tougher sell.

Strong regional graduate schools are an exception to this philosophy. Since most firms have regional offices, there is a good chance they'll go to a good local school, particularly if alums from the school work in that firm.

Experience

The section on work experience should be short on description and long on verifiable results. Think of this as the results section, rather than the experience section, of your resume. You should certainly mention the type of work you've done and the industries in which you have experience, but all in the context of what you've accomplished. If you can quantify the results of your work, you'll be better off. After all, it's all about the numbers.

Investment banks also care about the companies you've worked for. A measure of success, that is to say, a documented progression of roles and tasks at top companies is a plus, because performing well for them indicates to the resume reader that you have what it takes to survive in a competitive, rigorous environment of well-qualified peers. One insider tells us, "I am less inclined to focus on education and more inclined to focus on maturity—what have they done?"

If your experience is in a nontraditional business area, such as public sector, nonprofit, or other nonbusiness, you're going to have a tougher time. If your background isn't obviously business-related, you'll need to be much more specific about the results you have attained, and be clear about how such achievements will enable you to add value as a banker, sales person or trader.

If you have a nontraditional background, you should also keep in mind that individual firms have different levels of tolerance for and interest in attracting people from diverse backgrounds. To that end, you'll want to be sure to do your homework on each firm's hiring practices. You may also want to think about targeting regional or second-tier banks.

Other (or: Activities, Additional Information, Personal)

This section is your opportunity to tell the scanner a little more about yourself. Details typically include activities, interests, associations, memberships, and skills not already covered, such as proficiency in foreign languages. Such areas of your life may be relevant to how you will perform on the job—and relevance is the key. Remember, being successful in investment banking isn't only about crunching numbers and creating great PowerPoint presentations. You need strong communication skills and the ability to tolerate various personalities, ambiguity, and so on.

You can also use the Other section to mention activities that hint at gender, race, religion, sexual orientation, etc. You may have a slight advantage if your activities indicate that you fall into a group that a particular company is trying to recruit. This is a touchy subject, but many firms are desperate to recruit a varied work force to serve an increasingly diverse clientele. We constantly hear complaints from recruiters about how difficult it is to find diverse candidates. Therefore, highlighting your diversity could help your candidacy.

Insiders tell us that interesting or unusual information in this section can play a significant role in the decision to award an interview. However, we caution against using this section for frivolous information. Many people we interviewed said they had rejected otherwise decent resumes because of strange mentions in the Other section.

Formatting Guidelines for Resumes and Cover Letters

Stick with a format that's clean, error-free, and easy to read, and that clearly shows the two main sections: Education and Experience. Anything fancy is at best irrelevant, and at worst a negative factor that can result in a rejection letter. Remember, the format of your resume has one objective: to make your qualifications easy to understand. Conforming to standard resume format is generally seen as a good thing. Most business schools' career services offices provide a school standard. Stick to it!

When formatting your resume, you should adhere to the three Cs—clean, clear, conservative. While most resume reviewers don't have a specific model in mind, all seem to appreciate consistency. This generally means:

- A single, standard font: Times New Roman, Arial, Helvetica, or similar
- A readable font size: 11- or 12-point preferred, but no smaller than 10 point
- Neutral paper color: white or off-white
- Standard layout: no more than 1-inch, no less than 0.5-inch, margins, left aligned, line spaces between sections
- Clear resume organization: two or three sections labeled clearly, chronologic listing with dates, bulleted points making your resume more concise and easier to scan
- Clear letter organization: business format with one or two paragraphs, addressee name, company name, and date at the top

This also means you should resist the temptation to use excessive text formatting, graphics, or a matrix or graph. Such extras eat up space that could be dedicated to providing evidence of your qualifications, getting you additional checks or points, and helping you to land in the "call back" pile. Remember, cuteness may be perceived as desperation.

We can't stress the importance of bullets enough. Insiders tell us that reviewers are more likely to toss a resume into the ding pile than to spend extra time plowing through turgid, clunky prose to find what they're looking for. When you write bullets, remember to keep them short (one line if possible) and start them with action verbs.

Cover Letters

In investment banking recruiting, the cover letter is a little like a bull market—it's taken for granted until there's a problem. With that in mind, we recommend a low-risk strategy. The cover letter should be kept short and to the point, with a maximum length of one-half page. Don't rely on your cover letter to "fill in the gaps," or to put a customized spin on your experience. It's important that all your critical information be contained in your resume, because there's a good chance your cover letter won't be read. The cover letter should include the reason you are interested in the firm and the highlights of your resume that make you a good candidate for that firm. If you have a nonbusiness background, you might briefly explain why you are pursuing a career in investment banking. If you have a contact at the firm, mention that person.

Exceptions. There are a few cases in which cover letters are more important than indicated above. They are definitely more important when you send your resume to a firm directly, instead of through a campus recruiting program. In addition, insiders tell us that cover letters are used to assess candidates' ability to write clearly and concisely. Candidates with strong technical focus who might not be skilled writers, and international candidates whose first language is not English but who are seeking a position in the U.S., for example, undergo such scrutiny.

Do Your Due Diligence

Before writing a cover letter and submitting your resume to a firm, you should do your due diligence on the firm. Identify what about that firm specifically interests you. It may be an industry group or functional area specialty, its standing in the league tables or a discussion with a current employee that generated your interest in the firm. Whatever the case, make sure that what you write is accurate and shows that you've done your homework. You may want to purchase our detailed Insider Guides on specific top-tier firms. You can also find a list of current titles on our website at www.wetfeet.com.

Top Ten Things Interviewers Look for When Reviewing a Resume

10. A well-rounded candidate.
9. Something that makes you stand out from all the other Stanford/Harvard/Wharton graduates applying for this job.
8. A balance of work (or academic)/life experiences (as if bankers really know what that means!).
7. Experience in the industry of his current client and availability to be staffed immediately.
6. "You're assuming I actually get a chance to read resumes."
5. Someone who went to her alma mater. Not that she's biased.
4. "I'll know it when I see it."
3. An indication that the person is breathing.
2. Evidence that you'll be willing to spend every weekend in the office (without complaining).
1. A typo—so he can throw it out.

Preparing to Write

Before you begin writing your resume you must also scrutinize yourself. Which elements of your years of wisdom, experience, and accomplishment belong on a single sheet of paper, and which don't? What characteristics make you stand out from the crowd but also show that you're a team player? What kind of candidate does your target firm usually hire? This section will help you think through your activities and accomplishments and tell your compelling life story in one page.

Know Thy Audience

We can't stress enough the need to do your due diligence on the firms you are targeting. Almost every firm will ask the question, "Why us?" Make sure you can answer this question in an educated fashion. Think about what, specifically, might appeal to the recruiting team at your chosen firm. You may choose to include a reference in the cover letter. Look into the firm's noted areas of strength and focus, find out in which industries or product areas it excels. All of this information should influence the way in which you write your resume and cover letter, and especially the way in which you pursue an interview. Most firms have a website you can quickly check for some basic information.

WetFeet Resume Tip

Resume reviewers look favorably on candidates with backgrounds similar to their own. Read the employee profiles included in most firms' recruiting materials and websites and find someone who worked in the same company or attended the same school you did. You'll have a better chance of getting a favorable review.

Know Thyself

In addition to knowing all the factual information about yourself—grades, test scores, etc.—you need to think about how to portray yourself in a positive, confident light while telling the true story of who you are and what you've accomplished. You must have a good deal of insight into your experience, strengths, and weaknesses to create a compelling resume. The sources of inspiration for this vary. A few are noted below.

Academic records. Gather your school transcripts, standardized test scores, scholarship applications and awards, or any other information that may help you paint a picture of your academic capability. Calculate your GPA, because you'll probably need this information at some point. If you are concerned about your GPA, calculate it using several cuts—overall, major-only, by year, etc.—to see which provides the most favorable view to note on your resume or at least mention in the first interview. Also, be sure to use a standard 4.0 scale.

Recommendations. Re-read any recommendations written for you—for school, job or contest applications. Make note of the strengths mentioned. You should highlight these strengths as you describe your experience and accomplishments in your resume.

Performance reviews. Employer reviews may contain information on your rating vis-à-vis your peers. They may also include assessments of your accomplishments during your tenure. They are a good source of strengths and possibly of some quantitative results you've achieved in your career.

Employment history. If you don't already have one, prepare a chronological history of the major jobs you've held. Include the company names, your titles, your managers' names, the time you spent in those positions, your starting and ending salaries, and your primary responsibilities. This will be very useful in identifying upward trends in your career—increasing responsibility, increasing salary, or other advancement. Your employment history will also help you identify any gaps that will need to be accounted for on the resume or in the interview.

Review your top accomplishments. List the most significant accomplishments from your professional, academic, and personal lives. Write down each accomplishment, explain why it is significant to you, how you achieved it, how others helped you, and how you measure its success. You will need to include information about at least two of your top accomplishments in your resume, preferably with an indication of the results achieved.

Survey your strengths. Using the information above, think about the types of work or activities in which you have consistently succeeded—those situations in which you've performed well and felt good about it. The skills you used in these situations are most likely some of your strengths. Include evidence of these on your resume so the reader can identify you as a strong analyst, born leader, or formidable writer. These areas will likely be explored further in your interviews and you'll need to have thought through some examples from your resume.

Think about areas in which you could or should be stronger. You obviously won't highlight your weaknesses on your resume, but omission of information might prompt an interviewer to question you about these areas. If your resume lacks information on leadership positions, for example, you will need to show strengths in several other areas. It's a good idea to have thought through this before your interview anyway, because some interviewers still ask the old "what are your weaknesses?" question.

Showcasing Your Abilities

If you suspect that the only people who get investment banking interviews are those who have already been in the industry, you're partially correct. Certainly many firms are biased toward experienced bankers, salespeople, or traders who can "plug-in and go." And they are relatively safe in assuming that someone who has been in the job before has the skills and characteristics required to do the work. As everyone knows, the best indicator of future performance is past performance. However, firms continually have to bring in new talent as well (the turnover rate is much too high for firms to survive on industry veterans alone). Therefore, if you haven't worked for an investment banking firm in the past, you should try for the next best thing: demonstrating that you've done the same type of work, even if it was in a different context.

How can you do this if you've never been a banker, salesperson or trader? As discussed above, your resume reviewer will likely be looking for evidence of skills in several areas: quantitative/analytical ability, intelligence, drive for results, and teamwork. Think about the things you have done that will showcase your abilities in these areas. Below, we review some of the attributes most frequently sought by insiders. We have included a list of questions to help you identify work you have performed or activities you have pursued that will demonstrate your banking skills.

Quantitative/analytical ability. Quantitative or analytical skills are critical components of a banking resume. They are fundamental to your success as a banker, especially during the first few years. If you show no evidence of these skills, you will not get the interview. Expect to get tested for analytics in your interviews.

Have You:

- Filtered through data and assumptions and identified reasonable responses to complex problems?
- Synthesized large amounts of information and identified issues?
- Identified a problem and taken a proactive approach to solving it?
- Done well in courses with heavy analytical and quantitative content?
- Performed experiments that required formulation of a hypothesis and collection of evidence to prove or disprove it?

If so, you may have the analytical ability firms look for.

Drive for results. More and more firms are emphasizing results orientation in their hiring needs. Firms want to know whether you have the initiative, motivation, attention to detail, and energy necessary to deliver real results.

Have You:

- Brought new customers and revenue into your company?
- Proven yourself as a self-starter who goes above and beyond requirements?
- Shown the ability to switch priorities and move quickly among different tasks?
- Set a challenging goal and achieved it?
- Attended to the details while juggling multiple tasks (i.e. didn't let things fall through the cracks)
- Taken an innovative and efficient way to get something done?

If you haven't done any of these things or anything remotely similar, you might want to reconsider your desire to get into investment banking. These activities are part and parcel of all investment banking work, and your ability to perform well in a results-oriented environment will have a strong impact on your success at most firms. The need for rather specific, often quantitative measurements of your accomplishments should start you thinking about how to track and measure your achievements if you don't already.

Teamwork. Teamwork, with clients and peers, is a critical component of most, if not all, assignments. Investment bankers constantly work in teams—deal teams, sales teams, recruiting teams, and so on. Firms look for people who can work effectively with and inspire others toward a common goal.

Have You:

- Been a member of a sports team, study group, or committee?
- Worked effectively with people whose work style differs from yours?
- Inspired others to take action in an unstructured situation?
- Taken on the role of a team leader or player as needed?

Of course you have! We don't know of any candidate, particularly one at the business school level, who hasn't been involved in working with a team (love those study groups!). Identify the teams and/or groups you've been a part of (there is a difference between the two—teams form around a common goal) and think about the role you typically play. If you've proven your ability to play a productive role as a team member or, better yet, to effectively lead a team, highlight it. In your interview you may be quizzed on your team involvement, the type of role you tend to play on a team, or how you've worked with a team to identify and solve a problem.

Basic Resume Don'ts and Dos

So now you know the I-banker's preferred content and format, and you've done some soul-searching and come up with your perfect resume, right? Before you plaster it on electronic bulletin boards and send a mass mailing to every firm on the Street, check out and avoid the mistakes commonly found in resumes and cover letters. Some common resume mistakes can be turned into assets. Follow these tips for building a stronger, more refined resume:

Don't use vague qualitative terms such as "large" or "many," which leave the reader with questions about specifics.

Do use numbers where appropriate to clearly describe your accomplishments, as in "led a team of nine sales reps."

Don't waste resume space with frivolous information, such as "I like cheese."

Do include personal information that is relevant and gives the reader a better understanding of who you are.

Don't try to differentiate yourself with unconventional format or tactics such as graphics and colored paper.

Do stick to a basic, clear format that helps the reader glean information quickly and with minimal effort.

Don't try to portray yourself as a jack-of-all-trades in the hope that something will strike the reader's fancy.

Do discuss your two or three strengths and illustrate them with experience and achievement.

Don't get caught in the passive voice trap, writing as if things happened to you. "Went to Argentina to represent the firm …"

Do use the active voice with verbs that indicate you're in charge.

Don't even think of writing more than one page.

Do distinguish the important from the trivial in your background to fit the most relevant and significant elements onto a single page.

Mail Merge Morons and Other Big Offenders

We've talked a lot about what recruiters look for in resumes and cover letters. Well, there are also lots of things they don't like to see. If your resume fits one of these descriptions, you run a high risk of a ding, no matter how strong your background.

The mail merge moron. Mail merge morons send in their resume and cover letter to Merrill stating how much they would like to work for Lehman. As one insider tells us, "If they didn't take the time to even read their cover letter before sending it, how will they be able to produce flawless work once they're here?" Three words: proofread, proofread, proofread!

High inflation rates. Yeah, we know, everyone exaggerates to some extent, but insiders tell us that a resume that looks too good to be true probably is. Therefore, most of them look at a glowing resume with a heavy dose of skepticism. You need to sell yourself and showcase your talents without going overboard. The biggest mistake insiders say that job seekers make is the tendency to overstate experience. "I hate when candidates overstate their actual abilities. Then they get into an interview, and it's a joke. It comes out pretty quickly."

The title titillator. Title titillators think a fancy title will make their experience sound better. Consider the very impressive-sounding title "Director of Strategic Operations." What on earth does that mean? Any banker knows enough about how various industries are structured to be suspicious of such a title. Go with "Director of Business Development" instead. When in doubt, simplify so as to make your role and responsibilities clearer, rather than more obscure.

The liar. Frighteningly enough, many insiders we talked to said they had caught individuals lying about everything from what degrees they had earned to where they had earned them to where they had worked. One remembered a candidate from a top finance school who had lied about being fluent in five languages, one of which was Swedish. It so happened that his first-round interviewer was Swedish. When he began the interview in his native language, the candidate could only blush and admit to lying on his resume. Needless to say, he was not invited back for another interview.

Too much of a good thing. Resumes lacking focus are big losers. They include mentions of membership in seven different clubs without a leadership position in any of them; experience in five industries in the past four years; and knowledge of marketing, sales, manufacturing, finance, and information systems. Right!

Chek you're speling. "A typo is death," as one insider puts it. Typos will most likely get you thrown into the circular. Our insiders say one typo wouldn't disqualify a candidate, but several typos probably would. On the other hand, any typo is a good enough reason to nix a candidate, and depending on the reader's mood and level of patience, a typo might be just the excuse needed to whittle down that pile. Use your spell checker, but be sure to proofread carefully. Spell checkers won't catch all typos and won't check for other hazards such as misused contractions (your vs. you're, it's vs. its, etc.). It's always a good idea to have a friend or two read through your resume before you send it out. Remember, most reviewers are just looking for a reason to throw your resume into the ding pile.

Technology hang-ups. You may think e-mail is the best thing since the Pony Express, but that doesn't mean your recruiter does. Don't expect the person on the receiving end to fumble around with an attached file in a desperate quest to review your qualifications. If you have any doubts about the quality of the format in which your resume will arrive, because of platform or application variables, it's best to send a hard copy as well. Faxing is almost as fast as e-mail, and often more reliable, although it's definitely a good idea to follow up a faxed resume with a phone call to make sure it was received in legible form.

Buzzword Alert!

You need to sound business-savvy, to use current terms to describe your experience and abilities. How to select from the vast array of choices, and, most important, to avoid the banal buzzwords? Use the WetFeet Resume Terms guidelines, and you will sound professional and banking-oriented without seeming desperate.

Good, Solid Terms

These words (and their variations) are specific and quantitative without being too technical, and imply worthy accomplishments.

result	measure, ~ment
yield	model
analyze	forecast
manage	conduct
lead	implement
percent, ~age	process
revenue	create

Use with Caution

These terms often tip off a reader that the writer is trying to puff, embellish, or add gloss.

consult	sophisticated
strategy/strategic	complex
liaison	successful
recommend	facilitate
work with	co-anything
assist	

Buzzword Alert!

These words have become practically meaningless through overuse. Or they were never real words to begin with. Either way, you can be sure that in whatever context you use them they will be "wrong" to at least one reader. Our recommendation: Avoid them.

reengineering	change management
value chain	incentivize
methodological	

Resumes Reviewed

By this point you should have a pretty good idea of how an investment banking firm handles its resumes, and you should have started thinking about how to present your own qualifications. However, the final step remains. You have to take your basic package of skills and experience and turn it into a compelling marketing piece. To illustrate many of the points we have offered so far, and to give you ideas about how to improve your presentation, we have included four resumes and a sample cover letter. (We've changed the names and other revealing information to protect the guilty.) We selected an assortment of people from different backgrounds, and we reviewed them as applicants for an investment banking position.

Resume 1: MBA with Traditional I-Banking Background

JAMES JONES
110 Westwood Plaza, Box 951481
Los Angeles, CA 90095
310-825-1111
1 **jamesjones02@anderson.ucla,edu** 2

EDUCATION

The Anderson School at UCLA **Los Angeles, CA**
MBA, Concentration in Finance and Entrepreneurship June 2003
Memberships: Investment Banking Club, Finance Club, Entrepreneur Association, Anderson Real Estate Association
3 Service: Riordan Scholar Mentor, Challenge for Charity Organization
Sports Clubs: Squash, Golf, Ultimate Frisbee

4 **University of Pennsylvania Philadelphia, PA**
BA, English May 1998
3 Founding Member, Project Awareness: Organization dedicated to providing inner-city minority children with positive role models from the business community
Awarded Outstanding Freshman Sailor, Pennsylvania Sailing Team

EXPERIENCE

Merrill Lynch & Co. **New York, NY**
Summer Associate, Investment Banking 2002
5 Designed complex leveraged buyout, recapitalization, valuation, merger and debt capacity analysis for Merrill Lynch clients. Advised strategic and financial buyers on acquisitions, divestitures, restructurings and leveraged buyouts.

Donaldson, Lufkin & Jenrette Securities Corporation **New York, NY**
Financial Analyst, Mergers and Acquisitions Group 1998-2001
5 Drafted sales force marketing materials for debt and equity offerings. Prepared company calculations, including fairness opinions, based on discounted cash flow, comparable company, precedent transactions and break-up value analyses. Created leveraged buyout and merger models to assess pro forma effects of potential transactions on corporate earnings, capital structure, credit ratios and ownership. As a senior Analyst, managed and mentored first-year analysts. Led University of Pennsylvania recruiting team. 6
Modeling tutor for Analyst Training Program. Promoted to Associate February 2001.
7 Merger and Acquisitions transactions: $450 million sell-side advisory for client with spin-off of real estate
8 and aircraft assets to former management; $300 million buy-side advisory and placement agent for $20 million private convertible preferred equity security to fund the acquisition.

Financing transactions: $600 million senior notes offering; $68 million secondary equity offering; $50 million private exchange fund offering; $50 million preferred stock offering.

ADDITIONAL

Sailing: Private Yacht Captain; Sailing Instructor
Fluent in Spanish
Active volunteer for Special Olympics and Street Project

From Lost in Poor Formatting ...

This list refers to the numbered items in the resume on the opposite page:

1. Always include an e-mail address.
2. Oops. Small typos like this one can make a difference.
3. Clubs and Sports should be listed under Other/Personal.
4. Academic achievements?
5. Great experience gets lost in clunky text.
6. How many people did you manage?
7. How were you selected as the modeling tutor?
8. Good! Highlight a couple of transactions.

JAMES R. JONES

110 Westwood Plaza, Box 951481 ° Los Angeles, CA 90095 ° 310-825-1111
jamesjones02@anderson.ucla.edu

EDUCATION

Present — **The Anderson School at UCLA** — Los Angeles, CA

Candidate for Masters of Business Administration Degree, June 2003

- Concentration in Finance and Entrepreneurship

1994 - 1998 — **University of Pennsylvania** — Philadelphia, PA

Bachelor of Arts Degree, May 1998, magna cum laude

- Major in English
- Dean's List all semesters

EXPERIENCE

2002 — **Merrill Lynch & Co.** — New York, NY

Summer Associate, Investment Banking

- Designed complex leveraged buyout, recapitalization, valuation, merger and debt capacity analysis for Merrill Lynch clients.
- Advised strategic and financial buyers on acquisitions, divestitures, restructurings and leveraged buyouts.

1998-2001 — **Donaldson, Lufkin & Jenrette Securities Corporation** — New York, NY

Financial Analyst, Mergers and Acquisitions Group

- Drafted sales force marketing materials for debt and equity offerings.
- Prepared company calculations, including fairness opinions, based on discounted cash flow, comparable company, precedent transactions and break-up value analyses.
- Created leveraged buyout and merger models to assess pro forma effects of potential transactions on corporate earnings, capital structure, credit ratios and ownership.
- As a senior Analyst, managed and mentored 10 first-year analysts.
- Led University of Pennsylvania recruiting team.
- Selected by Analyst Steering Committee as modeling tutor for Analyst Training Program.
- Promoted to Associate February 2001.
- Merger and Acquisitions transactions: $450 million sell-side advisory for client with spin-off of real estate and aircraft assets to former management; $300 million buy-side advisory and placement agent for $20 million private convertible preferred equity security to fund the acquisition.
- Financing transactions: $600 million senior notes offering; $68 million secondary equity offering; $50 million private exchange fund offering; $50 million preferred stock offering.

PERSONAL

- Investment Banking Club, Finance Club, Entrepreneur Association, Anderson Real Estate Association
- Squash Club, Golf Club, Ultimate Frisbee Club, Private Yacht Captain; Sailing Instructor
- Fluent in Spanish
- Riordan Scholar Mentor, Challenge for Charity Organization, Special Olympics, Street Project

... To Clear and Concise

James has great experience in investment banking and a strong resume. However, at first glance, it's tough-going having to weed through his prose and get to the results. Our rewrite involves cleaning up the formatting in order to better highlight his achievements and his most significant responsibilities and accomplishments. The result is a resume that shows evidence of the basic banking skills (leadership potential, analytical skills, and some level of academic achievement), highlights specific accomplishments, and shows experience leading teams, analyzing data, and bringing about change in an organization. James now has a strong, balanced, and easy-to-read resume.

Resume 2: MBA with Traditional Sales and Trading Background

MERRILL MORGAN
Hinman Box 4000
Hanover, NH 03755
603-643-1000
merrillmorgan03@dartmouth.edu

EDUCATION

The Amos Tuck School of Business Administration **2001 – present**
Dartmouth College
❶ *Master of Business Administration*

University of Michigan **1992 - 1996**
❷ *Bachelor of Arts with Distinction, Economics and Japanese Studies*
Dean's List, Honors College, Sophomore Honors Award

EXPERIENCE

Lehman Brothers, Inc. **1998 - 2001**
Proprietary Trader, Listed Equities Division
❸
- Traded $100 mm in public securities on a monthly basis and consistently placed in top 5% in profitability for entire firm.
- Three year profit performance includes positive returns in 31 of 38 months including 29 of final 31 months of active trading.
- Generated over $1 mm in commissions for the firm and promoted to senior trader status after two years.
- Hired, trained and managed a group of eight proprietary traders. Training included equity valuations using fundamental research, buy/sell strategies, and market psychology.
- Trading activity included technical research analysis (e.g. price/volume divergence, momentum and flow charts) to determine optimal purchase and sell points for listed stocks.

J.P. Morgan Securities Corporation **1996 - 1998**
Fixed Income Analyst
❹
- Invested short-term cash management for accounts in excess of $80 million.
- Calculated forward rate information utilizing Excel for comparison with current discount rates, adding 75 basis points value for affected clients.
- Performed risk analysis of portfolios and proper asset allocation.
- Oversaw maintenance of portfolio management software.
- Executed all trades with institutional broker
- Researched on current trends, news and relevant economic information within the Capital Markets.
- Prepared current market rate information in domestic fixed income markets.
- Verified monthly pricing and yield information on client reports.

J.P. Morgan Securities Corporation **1997**
Summer Intern
- Performed analysis of stock list.
- Analysis assisted in a gain for branch office.

❺ **ADDITIONAL INFORMATION**
Licensed Series 7, Series 63 and Series 55
Interests include: downhill skiing, soccer ping-pong and investing

From Almost Perfect ...

This list refers to the numbered items in the resume on the opposite page:

1. Any academic achievement to show here?
2. This is great. Academic achievement is listed.
3. Good use of quantifiable results.
4. Good use of action verbs.
5. Please, no page two. Formatting can get this to one page.

MERRILL MORGAN

Hinman Box 4000 ° Hanover, NH 03755 °603-643-1000 ° merrillmorgan03@dartmouth.edu

EDUCATION

Present

The Tuck School of Business at Dartmouth College
Candidate for Master of Business Administration Degree, June 2004
- Tuck Scholar

1992 - 1996

University of Michigan
Bachelor of Arts with Distinction
- Double major in Economics and Japanese Studies
- Dean's List, Honors College, Sophomore Honors Award

EXPERIENCE

1998 – 2001

Lehman Brothers, Inc. New York, NY
Proprietary Trader, Listed Equities Division
- Traded $100 mm in public securities on a monthly basis and consistently placed in top 5% in profitability for entire firm.
- Three year profit performance includes positive returns in 31 of 38 months including 29 of final 31 months of active trading.
- Generated over $1 mm in commissions for the firm and promoted to senior trader status after two years.
- Hired, trained and managed a group of eight proprietary traders. Training included equity valuations using fundamental research, buy/sell strategies, and market psychology.
- Trading activity included technical research analysis (e.g. price/volume divergence, momentum and flow charts) to determine optimal purchase and sell points for listed stocks.

1996 – 1998

J.P. Morgan Securities Corporation Chicago, IL
Fixed Income Analyst
- Invested short-term cash management for accounts in excess of $80 million.
- Calculated forward rate information utilizing Excel for comparison with current discount rates, adding 75 basis points value for affected clients.
- Performed risk analysis of portfolios and proper asset allocation.
- Oversaw maintenance of portfolio management software.
- Executed all trades with institutional broker.
- Researched on current trends, news and relevant economic information within the Capital Markets.
- Prepared current market rate information in domestic fixed income markets.
- Verified monthly pricing and yield information on client reports.

1997

J.P. Morgan Securities Corporation Chicago, IL
Summer Intern
- Performed analysis of stock list.
- Analysis assisted in a gain for branch office.

ADDITIONAL INFORMATION

- Licensed Series 7, Series 63 and Series 55
- Interests include: downhill skiing, soccer ping-pong and investing

... To Stellar

Merrill had a near perfect resume. With the right packaging, he's sure to get several interviews with top firms. His strengths include a solid capital markets background, and good leadership and analytical skills. He showcases these strengths by using clear bullet points, employing action verbs and quantifying his results. Merrill took time to travel before business school. This gap is nearly undetectable on the resume and is so common that it can be left as is and explained in an interview. As you'll see on the next page, our edits are minor.

Resume 3: MBA with Nontraditional Experience

1 **Joseph Bell**
100 Darden Boulevard
Charlottesville, VA 22903
(434) 924-1111
josephbell03@darden.virginia.edu

2 Objective

Seeking a position in Corporate Finance.

3 Education

Darden Graduate School of Business Administration Charlottesville, VA
University of Virginia
Candidate for Masters of Business Administration, May 2003
4 Vice President of Finance Business Technology Club; Vice President of Black Business Student Association; Member of Venture Capital Club.

University of California Santa Cruz, CA
5 Bachelor or Arts in Politics, June 1998

Education

National Geographic Society, Washington, DC 1999 - 2001
Business Planning Manager

- Developed long-range strategic plans for magazines
- 6 Detected an error in budget and successfully worked with a team to formulate a solution that would minimize the impact on profit margin while maintaining circulation at budgeted levels.
- 7 Prepared circulation budget for magazine .
- Recognized interdepartmental communication breakdown. Acted as liaison between departments to implement a new system. 8
- Analyzed monthly variance from budget. Presented analysis and recommendations to Vice President of Circulation.

Price Waterhouse Coopers LLP, Washington, DC 1998-1999
Auditor

- Top-rated member of the 1998 Price Waterhouse – Washington, DC audit class.
- Developed an internal database and project profitability methodology to monitor the ongoing profitability of over $100 million of firm projects. 9
- Identified major follow-on project for major client and independently developed project proposal and methodology and prepared $400K project budget for senior management.Additional Information
- Major fundraiser for "Clinton for President" in 1992.
- Extensive foreign travel in over 22 countries including Honduras, Guatemala, Lebanon, Syria, Nepal, Thailand and Tibet.
- Hobbies include golf, skiing, and movies.

From Much to Prove ...

This list refers to the numbered items in the resume on the opposite page:

1. Consistent font, please!
2. Lose this. Adds no value.
3. Lose the borders.
4. Club activities should move to Other section
5. GPA? Honors? Academic achievements?
6. Size of error?
7. Size of budget?
8. "Liaison" is a dangerous word. What did you actually do?
9. What were the results?

Joseph Bell
100 Darden Boulevard/ Charlottesville, VA 22903/ (434) 924-1111
josephbell03@darden.virginia.edu

Education

2001-Present	Darden Graduate School of Business Administration University of Virginia Candidate for Masters of Business Administration, May 2003 GMAT: 730
1994 - 1998	University of California, Santa Cruz, CA Bachelor or Arts in Politics, June 1998 with honors Overall GPA: 3.8 ; Major GPA: 3.9

Experience

1999 – 2001

National Geographic Society Washington, DC

Business Planning Manager

- Developed long-range strategic plans for adventure magazines.
- Grew newly-launched magazine to nearly $4mm in revenue in one year.
- Managed team of 5 business analysts.
- Detected a $400K error in budget and successfully worked with a team to formulate a solution that would minimize the impact on profit margin while maintaining circulation at budgeted levels.
- Prepared circulation budget for magazine which had nearly one million subscribers and $12mm in circulation revenue.
- Identified inter-departmental communication breakdown. Led inter-departmental team to implement a new system.
- Responsible for ongoing management of newly created inter-departmental communication committee.
- Analyzed monthly variance from budget. Presented analysis and recommendations to senior management.

1998-1999

Price Waterhouse Coopers LLP Washington, DC

Auditor

- Designed activity based costing systems for clients to determine appropriate transfer process for contracts.
- Developed an internal database and project profitability methodology to monitor the ongoing profitability of over $100 million of firm projects, resulting in over $2 million in savings.
- Top-rated member of the 1998 Price Waterhouse – Washington, DC audit class.
- Identified major follow-on project for major client and independently developed project proposal and methodology and prepared $400K project budget for senior management.

Other

- Major fundraiser for "Clinton for President" in 1992.
- Extensive foreign travel in over 22 countries including Honduras, Guatemala, Lebanon, Syria, Nepal, Thailand and Tibet.
- Hobbies include golf, skiing, and movies.

... To Good Start

Joseph has a lot of explaining to do. He's coming from a second-tier undergraduate school and a nontraditional background. The first question most reviewers will ask is, "Why banking?" Joseph needs to emphasize his academic achievements and add some results to his work experience. Most important, he needs to start networking. His best chance of landing an investment banking interview is to use a contact. He should look for a UC Santa Cruz alumni and start there.

Resume 4: Basic Undergraduate

JANE DODD
Yale University
New Haven, CT 06520
203-432-1000
janedodd03@yale.edu

Education

YALE UNIVERSITY, New Haven, CT
BA Economics expected May 2003
❶ Major GPA 3.8
❷ *Coursework includes: Microeconomics, Macroeconomics, Portfolio Theory, Multi-Variable Calculus, Linear Algebra, Advanced Modern Chinese*

Experience

Jolsen Merchant Partners, San Francisco, CA — Summer 2002
Summer Analyst
❸ Created value by assisting in the structuring and finance of real estate acquisitions.
Worked closely with operating partner companies to analyze single asset and portfolio investments.
❹ Gained an understanding of finance, proprietary capital, and real estate opportunities worldwide.

Salomon Smith Barney, New York, NY — Summer 2001
Summer Intern
❺ Assisted financial consultant team in creating and executing marketing strategies in order to generate additional clients.
Reported asset allocation breakdown for financial consultants.

Economics Department, Yale University, CT — 2000 –present
Research Analyst
❻ Work with various professors on equity markets research.

Fine Foods, New Haven CT — 2000
Front End Manager
Supervise employees; interact with customers, responsible for bookkeeping.

Other

Yale Varsity Women's Crew 9/99-2/02
Yale Corinthian Yacht Club, Crew sailor 9/01 – present
Lived in Spain; fluent in written and spoken Spanish.
Volunteer, Big Sister Program.
Interests include fitness, Spanish literature, and Egyptology.

From Adequate ...

This list refers to the numbered items in the resume on the opposite page:

1. Great. Choose the calculation that gives the best result.
2. Excellent. Shows she can handle difficult course load.
3. Bullets, please.
4. Okay, but be prepared for extensive questioning on what exactly was learned.
5. What was your role?
6. How did you get this position?

JANE DODD
Yale University
New Haven, CT 06520
203-432-1000
janedodd03@yale.edu

Education

YALE UNIVERSITY, New Haven, CT
BA Economics expected May 2003
Major GPA 3.8
Coursework includes: Microeconomics, Macroeconomics, Portfolio Theory, Multi-Variable Calculus, Linear Algebra, Advanced Modern Chinese

Experience

Jolsen Merchant Partners, San Francisco, CA — Summer 2002
Summer Analyst
- Created value by assisting in the structuring and finance of real estate acquisitions.
- Worked closely with operating partner companies to analyze single asset and portfolio investments.
- Gained an understanding of finance, proprietary capital, and real estate opportunities worldwide.

Salomon Smith Barney, New York, NY — Summer 2001
Summer Intern
- Assisted financial consultant team in creating and executing marketing strategies in order to generate additional clients.
- Responsible for conducting market research.
- Reported asset allocation breakdown for financial consultants.

Economics Department, Yale University, CT — 2000 –present
Research Analyst
- Selected by professor to be sole student working with various professors on equity markets research.

Fine Foods, New Haven CT — Spring 2000
Front End Manager
- Supervised staff of 5 cashiers.
- Handled all customer comments and complaints.
- Responsible for bookkeeping.

Other

Yale Varsity Women's Crew 9/99-2/02
Yale Corinthian Yacht Club, Crew sailor 9/01 – present
Lived in Spain; fluent in written and spoken Spanish
Volunteer, Big Sister Program
Interests include fitness, Spanish literature, and Egyptology

To Impressive ...

Jane has done a good job of presenting her work experience. However, rather than being results-oriented, her bullets read like job descriptions. With a few minor additions, she was able to show that she is recognized by her professors as being academically successful. She also now shows herself as an academic leader and team player who is capable of juggling sports, work, and academics. In other words, perfect for investment banking.

Cover Letter Reviewed

Now we will take a look at a cover letter. Although the cover letter is less important than the resume, you'll want to be sure that you don't send something in that will eliminate you from consideration. The following example fills its role effectively.

Timothy J. Walinksy
110 Westwood Plaza
Box 951481
Los Angeles, CA 90095

September 10, 2002

Merrill Lynch, Inc.
Attention: Fritz Bracken
250 Vesey Street
23rd Floor
New York, NY 10281

Dear Mr. Bracken:

Joseph Rebas suggested that I forward my resume to you for your consideration. I am a second-year MBA student at the Anderson School at UCLA, and I am currently working as a summer associate at J.P. Morgan in New York.

As Joseph may have mentioned, I am in the top 5% of my class at Anderson, and I was recently elected President of the Investment Banking Club. In and out of the classroom I have consistently demonstrated my capacity to make a positive impact regardless of the situation. My analytical and personal skills are ideally suited to investment banking, and I am confident that I would be an asset at Merrill Lynch.

I will call you next Wednesday to discuss next steps. If you do have any questions regarding my resume or qualifications, please do not hesitate to call me at 310-825-1000. I look forward to speaking with you.

Sincerely:

Tim Walinsky

This is a very solid letter—clear, concise, and direct. We recommend that Tim try to reach Fritz in person. He should call him a few days after the expected arrival of his cover letter and resume. He can leave a voice mail message, though that puts him at risk of initiating a game of phone tag, which can be frustrating for both parties. Bill should also check grammar carefully. Sticklers would note the improper use of the preposition "at" after the word asset. The proper wording is "I would be an asset to Merrill Lynch."

Now you have all the tools to create a great resume. Grab that keyboard (or pen and paper) and start working!

Getting Your Foot in the Door

Now that you have a great resume, what should you do with it? Investment Banking firms receive resumes through three primary channels: campus recruiting programs, employee recommendations, and "over the transom"—directly from a candidate, unsolicited or in response to an ad. Insiders tell us that your chances of getting an interview vary significantly depending on which channel you use. But whatever the channel, timing is very important. It's best to investigate the firm's recruiting cycle, which usually gears up around September and October for full-time hires or January for summer hires. This is when firms are most likely hiring and determining the headcount they'll need the following year.

Campus Recruiting

The best way to get into a firm is to go through the campus interviewing process. All top firms purchase resume books from graduate schools and select candidates to interview from those. They also interview on many campuses. Most firms actively recruit at the top colleges and business schools. These days firms are very anxious to get the best and brightest people, and since they are already expending the energy to come to a campus to interview candidates, they feel they should interview as many as possible. If you aren't selected by the firm for an interview, bid what points you must to obtain an interview. If the firm you're targeting does recruit on your campus, it's a good idea to attend the information sessions usually offered a few weeks before interviews. Many insiders we spoke with say they are more likely to spend extra time reading a resume and even giving the benefit of the doubt to a candidate who has expressed interest in the firm by attending events and making an effort to meet some of the team members there. Additionally, you can use the information session and other events as an opportunity to start proving your communication skills. Getting a check in that box of the Big Four characteristics will put you ahead of the game when resumes are reviewed.

Personal Contact

If you're not currently in school, or if you are, but not at one where firms recruit, you're going to have a greater challenge on your hands. Insiders unanimously agree that your best bet is to try to find someone you know at the firm or someone who has a contact at the firm. Look into your school alumni directories to see if any graduates are working there. Or get a contact name in the industry or product group in which you have relevant experience. Call the switchboard and ask for names if you must.

The best route is to call the contact person, give him or her your 15-second resume summary, and ask for information about the firm. You have two objectives in doing this: to get more information on the firm to use in your interview, and to get that person to ask for your resume so he or she can forward it to the right person. Once you have a contact, send your resume to that person. Ideally, the contact will forward the resume to the person who reviews resumes and schedules interviews, with a note asking that an interview be granted.

With a strong resume and a recommendation, you're probably a shoo-in. Insiders tell us that an employee recommendation strongly affects the decision to interview a candidate. Though we don't have statistics, all agree that your chances of getting an interview through a personal contact go way up, even if your resume is less than stellar.

Over the Transom

If you strike out in the personal contact arena, your resume really counts. It's the only tool you have to sell yourself, and it represents your only chance to get a foot in the door. When submitting your resume, whether in response to a job listing or without solicitation, target firms that are likely to be interested in your background. Your resume will most likely be screened by an administrator for the Big Four characteristics, then forwarded to a recruiter in the specific practice area. Specialization, to the greatest extent possible, is probably your best angle. You have a better chance of getting an interview if someone with a similar background, who has needs in your area of expertise, reads your resume.

Following Up

Do not become a nuisance, but do be persistent. After all, many firms look for people who take initiative and are good problem solvers.

Here are a few basic rules for following up once you've sent your resume:

- Be persistent but not pesky—two calls in one day are overkill; two calls in one week are probably fine.
- Be prescriptive in your requests—ask specifically for what you want, whether it's to schedule an interview or have a casual chat on the phone.
- Keep the ball in your court—you'll probably feel more in control if you can plan the next steps rather than wait by the phone.
- Make yourself easily available—provide a number where a message can be left at any time; if possible, plan to travel to the firm's office for a meeting at your expense.

The Phone Fandango

You don't want to get into a game of phone tag with an investment banker. You will lose every time. Insiders tell us that one of the most difficult things to do is return phone calls while working on a deal. Put yourself in the shoes of the average investment banker, trader, or salesperson with recruiting responsibility. You're working 100 hours on a merger or stuck at your trading desk all day as the market goes wild . . .

Here's what happens when an associate in M&A listens to your voice mail on Wednesday at 11:59 p.m.:

You: This is Merrill Morgan calling on Wednesday at 10:00 a.m. I sent you my resume on Monday and wondered whether you'd had a chance to take a look at it. I'll be in all day today, at 333-555-8956.

Associate thinks: Who is Merrill Morgan, and why is he calling me?

He has certainly not seen the resume—he hasn't even been in the office since last Friday. And he surely doesn't have time to return your call without committing a time-zone foul. When he finally gets a few minutes free with access to a phone, he's more likely to call his significant other or pet poodle than to return a phantom resume call. Most likely your voice mail gets deleted without much more thought.

Message Magic

If you plan to call, here is a better approach:

You: This is Merrill Morgan calling on Wednesday. I'm an MBA candidate from Fuqua with experience in the M&A group at UBS. At John Smith's request, I sent my resume to you on Monday. I would like to schedule an interview and will call you on Friday to discuss my qualifications.

Associate thinks: Hmm, I remember this resume, and it's probably worth seeing him. I'll call John to get more information before he calls me back on Friday.

In this case, you left a brief message with some information on your background so the associate would remember seeing the resume. You were specific about your plans to call back on Friday, which gives him an opportunity to check with John Smith.

If you've left a message, and your call hasn't been returned, don't hesitate to call again. Remember, investment bankers are usually fully booked during the day and often work late into the night, when the last thing on their minds is returning resume calls. The best tactic is to be persistent and pleasant without badgering. Most insiders we spoke with say they usually make an effort at least to return a call, even if they aren't interested in interviewing the candidate. Don't give up until you've tried at least three times over two weeks to contact the recruiter.

If you've left three messages and all have been ignored, you may want to send your resume to someone else and start the process again. Another option is to contact a recruiting coordinator or the banker's assistant if one exists, and determine the best method of contacting your target. Many firms communicate primarily through voice mail, although you might have luck using e-mail or even leaving a good old-fashioned message with the secretary. Tailor your approach to what you have learned about how that particular firm communicates.

Note: If you don't reach the banker, your treatment of the recruiting coordinator or secretary should be positive and respectful. Treat any person at the firm the same way you would the professional responsible for reviewing your resume. We know of more than one candidate rejected by the recruiting coordinator because of an attitude!

Interview Prep

Many insiders tell us they develop interview questions according to experience mentioned on a candidate's resume. The best way to prepare for the first interview is to know your resume extremely well. Develop and practice a 20- to 30-second pitch that summarizes your experience and major achievements You will use this countless times, especially in interviews for sales and trading positions, to introduce yourself over the phone or in an interview when the interviewer has not had a chance to review your qualifications. Preparing your pitch will help you articulate the items listed on your resume. You should be able to describe points on your resume in a clear, concise, and convincing manner. You should also be prepared to discuss each area of your Experience section, providing details and insight wherever possible.

Resume Watchouts

As we have mentioned, your resume will help the interviewer identify areas to probe during the first interview. In particular, interviewers will look for weaknesses or inconsistencies to check, and may even formulate questions directed at your resume weaknesses. Read your resume with a critical eye, looking for things that might appear odd or inconsistent. Use the list below to help you identify those areas that are of particular concern to interviewers.

Time gaps. One reason interviewers like chronological resumes is that they want to know whether a candidate took time off between school years or jobs. Time off is not necessarily a bad thing, but you need to be prepared to explain any lapses between jobs or between your sophomore and junior year, for example. If you traveled, be prepared to describe something you learned during that time. If you took time off to have a baby, resolve a personal issue, or "find yourself," you need to practice your answer to the time gap question. It's usually best not to go into a lot of personal detail—insiders tell us this is a warning sign, especially in the first interview. But be clear and focus on what you accomplished during that time. Firms want to be sure you can handle the normal rigors of four or more years in academia, jobs with increasing responsibility, and balancing your personal and professional lives.

Inconsistent performance. If your accomplishments appear strong in one area and weak in another—1400 on the SATs with a 3.2 GPA, honors graduate of a top school with no notable professional accomplishments—you should expect questions about this disparity. The interviewer will want to know the reason behind your low GPA (did you work part time during school?) or your mediocre experience. Be prepared to explain any circumstances that impacted your performance, but again, avoid undue personal detail.

Job hopping. If you've been at several companies in just a few years, or never stayed at one company longer than a year or two, you risk being perceived as a job-hopper. Your interviewer may wonder whether you've been fired for poor performance. Frequent career changes sometimes indicate that a person has difficulty sticking with a situation, working through problems, or committing to a job. All of these are obvious concerns to investment bankers, whose work requires tenacity and a strong commitment to delivering client value. In addition, most firms look for people who want to stay around for a while. Three years is often considered a breakeven point, but many firms would like individuals with longer-term tenure in mind.

Local yokels. If you've spent most of your academic and professional life in Boston, you may be questioned about your sudden interest in joining the Chicago office of a firm. This is especially true for those who have attended school and worked in California. Midwest and East Coast firms have a terrible time getting these candidates to relocate, and in some cases they have all but given up trying. A firm that must fly you out for an interview will probably quiz you over the phone before anteing up.

Next Steps

1. Check out investment banking Company Profiles at www.wetfeet.com.
2. Browse the WetFeet.com store for our Insider Guide to *Careers in Investment Banking* as well other Insider Guides to top I-banking firms.

WetFeet's Insider Guide Series

Ace Your Case! The WetFeet Insider Guide to Consulting Interviews
Ace Your Case II: Fifteen More Consulting Cases
Ace Your Case III: Practice Makes Perfect
Ace Your Case IV: The Latest and Greatest
Ace Your Interview! The WetFeet Insider Guide to Interviewing
Beat the Street: The WetFeet Insider Guide to Investment Banking Interviews
Getting Your Ideal Internship
Get Your Foot in the Door! Landing the Job Interview
Job Hunting A to Z: The WetFeet Insider Guide to Landing the Job You Want
Killer Consulting Resumes!
Killer Cover Letters and Resumes!
Killer Investment Banking Resumes!
Negotiating Your Salary and Perks
Networking Works!: The WetFeet Insider Guide to Networking

Career and Industry Guides

Accounting
Advertising and Public Relations
Asset Management and Retail Brokerage
Biotech and Pharmaceuticals
Brand Management
Health Care
Human Resources
Computer Software and Hardware
Consulting for Ph.D.s, Lawyers, and Doctors
Entertainment and Sports
Industries and Careers for MBAs
Industries and Careers for Undergrads
Information Technology

Investment Banking
Management Consulting
Marketing and Market Research
Non-Profits and Government Agencies
Oil and Gas
Real Estate
Top 20 Biotechnology and Pharmaceutical Firms
Top 25 Consulting Firms
Top 25 Financial Services Firms
Top 20 Law Firms
Venture Capital

Company Guides

Accenture
Bain & Company
Bear Stearns
Booz Allen Hamilton
The Boston Consulting Group
Cap Gemini Ernst & Young
Citigroup
Credit Suisse First Boston
Deloitte Consulting
Goldman Sachs
IBM Business Consulting Services
JPMorgan Chase
Lehman Brothers
McKinsey & Company
Merrill Lynch
Monitor Group
Morgan Stanley